THE
MARRIAGE DECALOGUE

*10 Practical Steps to Progress Through the
Dynamic Stages of Marriage*

Howai K Thomas

The Marriage Decalogue
Copyright © 2025 by Howai K Thomas

ISBN: 979-8992725421 (sc)
ISBN: 979-8992725438 (e)

Mission Wholelife Publications
941-467-0946
missionwholelifepublications.com
info@missionwholelifepublications.com

Table of Contents

PROLOGUE

One significant thing we have in common is relationships. Whether family, friends, business, academic, religious, or romantic relationships, we all desire to connect with people with whom we can share laughter, friendship, work, caring, and support through the good times and the hard times in life.

Relationships are formed out of various life dynamics. Many people who form lifelong relationships, like marriage, say they did so because they love each other. But what is love? How would you define it?

If you were to do a quick Google search on your desktop computer or mobile device, you would find that there are many types of love, including Agape (selfless love), eros (romantic love), infatuation love at first sight), ludus (childish or playful love), mania (obsessive love), philia/phileo (friendship love), philautia (self-love), pragma (enduring love), storge (family love), and the list goes on.

How ever many types or levels of love there are, our lives are riddled with this four-letter word: LOVE. "Love has a prominent role in thousands of books, songs, magazines, and movies. Numerous philosophical and theological systems have made a prominent place for love. Psychologists have concluded that the need to feel loved is a primary human emotional need.

1

For love, we will climb mountains, cross seas, traverse desert sands, and endure untold hardships."[1]

What would you do, or not do for love?

Perhaps only some of what I just said applies to you. But imagine with me, for a moment, that you are about to witness the wedding of two people who decided to get married because they are in-love with each other, and they want to spend the rest of there lives together.

Imagine you are there when the following words were said: "Dearly beloved, we are gathered here today to celebrate the marriage of David Newlywed and Monique Newbride." At which moment, all their family, friends, and guests are gathered around in support of them. All filled with anxiety, excitement, and hopefulness, and can hardly wait to hear the declaration: "I now pronounce you husband and wife; you may kiss your bride!"

But without good counsel (instructions or guidance), any endeavor, including marriage, will fail.[2]

Prior to this point of trying to "tie the knot," David and Monique courted for a while; they had gone to premarital counseling. For in the multitude of good counsel, there is wisdom, safety, and plans can better be established; but without good counsel (instructions or guidance), any endeavor, including marriage, will fail.[2]

Here are some of the things David and Monique had a chance to go over during courtship and especially during their premarital counseling sessions.

They discussed finances, sleeping routines, eating habits, educational interests and pursuits, mutual and personal goals, family planning, religious beliefs, conflict resolution, roles and responsibilities, and each other's social circles.

You see, we invest a lot of time and resources into planning weddings, but how much planning and resources do we invest in the marriage itself?

I know some of these may not seem significant to some people, but two can't walk together in oneness unless they have a common agreement,[3] and these are the things, typically, conflicts have in common.

For some more elaboration on some of these, read chapters 2 and 3 of my book *The Baby Analogy of Marriage.*

Though David and Monique are an imaginary couple, they illustrate the ideal approach real couples should take toward marriage, and many have. You see, we invest a lot of time and resources into planning weddings, but how much planning and resources do we invest in the marriage itself?

After being married for more than fifteen years, this is something I am still learning more about and still need more improvement on. Lack of marital investment is also among the reasons why the divorce rate is so high, *especially* if the lack is emotional, financial, and quality-time spending. I don't think anyone in their right mind gets married to fail, but I've learned that if marriage is going to work out, we have to plan for, invest in, and work out our marriage.

While this is not a book of dos and don'ts, nonetheless, I've included some dos and don'ts that we commit or fail to commit, which either build up or break down the marriage bonds.

My goal in this book is to share biblical yet practical principles to help you progress through the five stages of marriage.

This is the same journey that I've been on for sixteen years, but more recently, I've learned more about these key principles, and I hope they'll be a "game changer" for you and your marriage.

Finally, though this book contains and elaborates on certain vital relational concepts and principles, it serves as an introduction to the greater wealth of material available to help us grow and develop in our marriage relationships.

SECTION A: The Five Stages of Marriage

We humans go through different stages of development—a child grows through various psychological and physiological changes during youth and teenage years into a mature adult male or female. Then, we not only see the world through different lenses, but we experience it differently too.

In this stage, we tend to dismiss other's perspective of our newfound love that doesn't agree with ours.

Likewise, marriages go through different stages of development. Generally speaking, it is noted that married couples will go through five different stages, but not all go through them in the very same way or to the same degree of intensity. Let's explore these "five stages of marriage."[4]

First Stage: In-Love Experience/Enchantment Stage

On December 20, 2018, *USA Today* featured an article about a couple who are on "the world's longest honeymoon." Their names are Mike and Anne Howard, and they have documented their accomplishments in their travels on their website honeytrek.com.[5] From their website, we read the following:

> Using Anne's background as a magazine editor and Mike's as a digital media strategist and photographer, we started our couples travel blog to share our seven-continent journey and inspire

more people to follow their far-flung dreams. HoneyTrek has grown to be a leading travel blog with over 375,000 followers and has received acclaim from hundreds of media outlets—from *USA Today* to *Lonely Planet*. National Geographic even took notice of our crazy journey and asked us to write their first book on couples' adventure travel, Ultimate Journeys for Two. We're proud to say it's a bestseller and published in four languages. To write our newest book and explore our own continent, we bought a vintage RV (aka Buddy the Camper) and set out on a two-year, nine-country, 73,000-mile quest to find the best glamping experiences in North America. The result is Comfortably Wild, an award-winning guidebook and the first ever written on this trending travel style.[6]

As you can expect, these behaviors engender and intensify conflicts, even though conflicts are common to human relationships.

This is certainly not the typical married couple or married life. However, they, like the typical married couple, would start out with the in-love experience or the enchantment stage.

This is the stage when emotions are high—you're on cloud nine. You are excited, happy, helpful, and hopeful. In this stage, we tend to dismiss other's perspective of our newfound love that doesn't agree with ours.

We also gloss over minor differences, even "red flags." This is the stage where you also look at each other idealistically and are careful not to hurt each other's feelings. As you "endeavor to keep the unity of the spirit in the bonds of peace,"[7] you express kindness, tenderheartedness, and forgiveness toward each other. You even forgo your own desires or preferences to minimize conflicts in your attempt to keep a good thing going. Inevitably, after the wedding and the honeymoon, this euphoria calms down, and sometime after that, we get to the second stage.

Second Stage: Disappointment/Disenchantment Stage

After the wedding ceremony and honeymoon are over, there is a tendency for disappointment or disenchantment to set in. We have different thoughts and experience different emotions as we seek to fulfill our new roles and responsibilities. Unfortunately, these sometimes express themselves in anger, unkind words, invalidation, insensitivity, indifference, power struggles, mind over-mind control, and manipulation. As you can expect, these behaviors engender and intensify conflicts, even though conflicts are common to human relationships.

Of course, such circumstances are the results of our own attitudes, actions, and choices, and not God's doing.

Often, people think their personality differences or upbringing bring the most conflict into their relationships.

Still, how well we do or don't handle these differences makes or breaks the bonds between us; not the conflicts themselves.

"This doesn't mean that differences don't matter. They can be part of what draws two people together and also part of what makes it difficult, at times, to get along. But the part of this over which you have the most control is how the two of you handle whatever differences you have. If you want to have a great relationship, the way you handle differences can matter more than what those differences are."[8]

In getting through or enduring this stage of marriage and resolving marital conflicts, spouses may even wonder if they've made a mistake in marrying. They may even think about the counsels they've negated and neglected. Some Christian couples even question or lose faith in God. They may say something like, "God, why did you let me do this?" or, "God, your Word says, 'He who finds a wife finds a good thing,'"[9] or, "Lord, your Word says you would 'give me the desires of my heart if I commit myself, wait and put my trust in you.'"[10] Of course, such circumstances are the results of our own attitudes, actions, and choices, and not God's doing.

The thoughts and feelings experienced and expressed during the second stage aren't uncommon in relationships but need to become less common and less frequent to maintain harmony and happiness. This is a goal that we should   First, don't stop fighting for and working on your marriage.

all strive to achieve. Many have achieved this goal, have made it through this disappointment stage, through the third stage (which we are about to look at), and have gone on to the "friendship" and "mature love" stages.

However, before talking about those other stages, I would like to pause to encourage you to press forward and not give up if you're in the second stage, the third stage, or any other stage of marriage. Here are three suggestions to help you get through: First, don't stop fighting for and working on your marriage.

Third, do not keep yourselves from each other or seek emotional fulfillment in anything or anyone else, whether physical or virtual (like drinking, drugs, gambling, flirting, pornography, or any other vice to find "relief").

Don't think that your marriage should or will automatically work out because you love each other or have a high compatibility rate; that's a myth.

Second, be all you can be for your husband or wife. Things don't get better if you display your worst attitudes and behaviors; they only get worse. While your partner doesn't get everything right, still express gratefulness and thankfulness for what they do. This helps your heart remain tender and open toward each other. If both of you are hardheaded and hardhearted, then you'll give each other headaches and heartaches by butting heads continually. But if your spouse is violent and abusive, talk to someone who can help. On the other hand, if *you're* violent or abusive, go get help before it's too late.

Third, do not keep yourselves from each other or seek emotional fulfillment in anything or anyone else, whether physical or virtual (like drinking, drugs, gambling, flirting, pornography, or any other vice to find "relief").

If you do, these will destroy trust and push you further into frustration and depression. This will also slowly erode the emotional foundation and security of your relationship and erect more emotional barriers between you two, further weakening your bonds and leading you to express contempt for each other. All of these invite infidelity into the marriage. Still, though, whatever actions you commit is a choice on your part, regardless of how the marriage turns out.

Now, let's get back on track with talking about the third of the five stages of marriage.

Third Stage: Obligation/ "Settling" Stage

In this stage, several dynamics occur: couples grow weary from fighting. All the power struggles and manipulative maneuvers have only resulted in more anger, bitterness, frustration, and resentment. They've yet to succeed in changing each other.

"Marriage is not a lifelong Springtime," he says, "But we can come back to the optimism, enthusiasm, and enjoy Spring many times in the course of our lives.

The things they once enjoyed doing for each other are now done out of obligation or mere duty. They settle in dismay: "It is what it is." "Que sera, sera" (whatever will be, will be), they say. Though dissatisfied, unhappy, and unfulfilled, they want to maintain their commitment to the marriage—their vows to each other before God and man. They want to do the right thing, and deep down inside, they want the marriage to work out, even though, at times, they are not sure it can.

This stage reminds me of a statement in Gary Chapman's book about the seasons married couples go through: "Marriage is not a lifelong Springtime," he says, "But we can come back to the optimism, enthusiasm, and enjoy Spring many times in the course of our lives.

We'll inevitably have our seasons of summer, fall, and Winter as well, though not necessarily in that predictable order. As mentioned earlier, the seasons of marriage are not chronological, and thus springtime is not exclusively for newlyweds. The seasons repeat themselves numerous times throughout a marriage, and because we are creatures of choice, we can create new beginnings whenever we desire."[11]

So there is hope for anyone caught in what may seem like a hopeless situation—an endless fall or a never-ending winter.

Both the fourth and fifth stages of marriage are about hope and living out the "spring" and "summer" time of marriage. Now, let's take a look at these two final stages.

Fourth Stage: "Friendship Love"/In-Love Again Stage

One notable virtue children often display is their ability to make up after a fight. If anyone truly displays what it means to "let not the sun go down on your anger,"[12] it would be them.

The "friendship stage" is about rekindling and fanning the "flames" of love. One of the crucial steps taken to get to this stage is applying a counsel Jesus gave to the church (His "bride") when she fell out of love with Him. "Remember therefore from where you have fallen, and repent and do the first works."[13] Married couples whose marriages experience a "rebirth," remember when they first started out—the intense emotions they felt for each other. They were curious about each other and desired to see, hear, and spend time together; they expressed tender regard and affection toward each other and the things they hoped to do and accomplish together. They were quick to forgive and willing to please each other.

In other words, to move from the "obligation stage" into the "friendship stage," they had to have a change of heart, mind, and attitude and do those "first works" they did in the beginning stages of their relationship. To move from the "obligation stage" into the "friendship stage" also means they had gone from being resentful, regretful, remorseful, and retaliatory to being redemptive, apologetic, and forgiving.

This change of attitude fosters peacemaking; peacemaking makes room for reconciliation and makes it safe to connect and do right by each other. As one Bible writer said, "The fruit of righteousness," or right doing, "is sown in peace of them that make peace."[14]

In chapter 3, I talked about the wave of emotions and bonding interactions between mothers and children. When married couples go back to the first works, they are, in a sense, returning to the "baby stage."

While working on a piece of network equipment at a bank, the manager I was talking with told me that she believes the empty-nest years are where this type of friendship could be experienced. She thinks this is because the husband and wife are left alone, and their lives no longer involve parenting responsibilities. However, I've learned that married folks stay together during this period if they've bonded well during the years before becoming empty nesters.

To move from the "obligation stage" into the "friendship stage" also means they had gone from being resentful, regretful, remorseful, and retaliatory to being redemptive, apologetic, and forgiving.

Whether you experience this stage prior to or during the empty-nester years, one thing is for sure: friendship requires that the two be friendly, for those who are to have friends must show themselves to be friendly.

Think about how children make friends: they approach with a non-threatening gesture—a wave of the hand to say hi, then, followed by a personal inquiry— what's your name, or do you want to play? Before long, they are talking, sharing, laughing, and playing with each other.

Many preschool experts say that playing is the work children need to do. Through play, children gain developmentally relevant social, emotional, and cognitive abilities. We believe the developmental importance of play doesn't die

To "strengthen the things which remain that are ready to die" requires that you "don't throw out the baby with the bathwater."

after childhood, but continues throughout life. Fun and play allow a release of oneself from all the pressures and hassles of being an adult. The relaxed togetherness of playful times is important in the initial development of the bond between two people. That's because when we are engaged in fun through play, we're often relaxed and more ourselves. It's under these conditions that people fall in love—when one sees in the other a relaxed self in the context of fun times together.[15]

Another biblical counsel that is very helpful in transitioning out of the "obligation stage" to this fourth stage of marriage is to "strengthen the things which remain that are ready to die."[16]

I've heard it said by someone whom I don't remember that we live in a "throw-away culture." If something is broken that can be repaired, instead, we throw it away and get a brand-new one, whether we can afford it or not. To "strengthen the things which remain that are ready to die" requires that you "don't throw out the baby with the bathwater."

In other words, you don't take the minor fixable issues that aren't detrimental to the relationship and make them a major. Which things can make you feel as though your partner is not uniting, cooperating, harmonizing, or supporting you, and then you give up.

"Life and death are in the power of the tongue."

Instead of thinking and feeling that way, give it a fighting chance—work on fixing the fixable problems that emotionally separate you two from becoming closer, especially the little things which add up and can become volcanic.

As you do so, be empathetic, have your speech "seasoned" with grace, and be kind one to another, tender-hearted, forgiving one another.[17] By doing this, you can revive that "love and feeling" you once had for each other, especially if it had gone cold.

In addition, think of your love as a growing plant that must be cultivated and nourished. In a practical sense, like you would grow a plant in a garden, by braking up the soil around it so air and sunlight can get in, by adding mulch or fertilizer, and by giving it water so it can survive and thrive, so you have to infuse your relationship with things that promote its life.

One way to do this is to pay attention to your words and how you speak to your spouse. "Life and death are in the power of the tongue,"[18] and you can use your words to give your relationship life or death.

"Everything we say is either a bomb or a balm. Bombs destroy. Balm is an aromatic oil or ointment that is soothing and healing. Harsh, cruel, condemning words are like bombs exploding in the hearts of the recipient. Kind, loving, affirming words are like an ointment of healing to the heart of the one who receives them."[19]

Every time my wife and I have a "good talk," things always feel better, and fewer emotional barriers are built between us, which, in turn, strengthens our bonds and increases intimacy.

"Affectionate hearts, truthful, loving words, will make happy families and exert an elevating influence upon all who come within the sphere of their influence."[21]

I believe that couples who have gotten to the "friendship stage" have learned to have their speech "seasoned" with grace,[20] and speak more "verbal balms" instead of "verbal bombs."

This will not only breathe new life into our hearts, homes, and relationships, but also positively impact others we relate to. For "Affectionate hearts, truthful, loving words, will make happy families and exert an elevating influence upon all who come within the sphere of their influence."[21]

Fifth Stage: Mature Love/Going Strong and Steady

When a child passes through the various developmental stages into adulthood, much has changed with how they feel, view, and experience life. Similarly, when a husband and wife attain mature love, they feel, view, and experience life together in a different way too:

They've come through the vicissitudes of life together and are mutually submitted to each other.

Their love doesn't die away, even though severely tested.

With deep conviction and commitment, they are honoring their marriage vows.

Duties/responsibilities are a delight and not a chore or drudgery.

They have head-to-heart communication instead of hardheaded conversations (arguments, combativeness, defensiveness, and monologues).

They choose to resolve conflicts and not dissolve them.

Also, if your marriage is going to work out, then you have to work out your marriage.

Now, they collaborate and not just accommodate each other; they choose not to abdicate responsibilities, dictate to, or manipulate each other to get their way.

They've learned how to play and have fun with each other.

Their relationship more reflects the love portrait of 1 Corinthians 13:4–7, which says, "Love is patient and kind; love does not envy or boast; it is not arrogant or rude. It does not insist on its own way; it is not irritable or resentful; it does not rejoice at wrongdoing, but rejoices with the truth," a love that is forbearing, hopeful, and enduring.

Once again, your marriage may or may only go through some of these stages to the same extent other marriages do. Also, if your marriage is going to work out, then you have to work out your marriage.

Also, if your marriage is going to work out, then you have to *work out* your marriage.

Sure, this is easier said than done, but it can be done, has been done, and is being done by many others.

SECTION B: The Marriage Decalogue (10 Practical Steps to Progress Through the 5 Stages)

1. Marriage is a team of two. (Genesis 1:27; Matthew 19:4-5; Ephesians 5:22–31; Philippians. 2:3-4; Hebrews 13:3)

Have you ever heard the saying, "Teamwork makes the dream work"? Many people dream of finding a lifelong companion, getting married, starting a family, and living happily ever after. While for many this is a dream come true; unfortunately, for many others, after the wedding or the honeymoon is over, they wake up to nothing short of a nightmare.

By comparison, marriage is a team of two. It was instituted by God and, among other things, requires mutual honor, mutual respect, mutual submission, love, and sacrifice to make it to the "finish line," and win together.

It is common knowledge that for any competing team to win against their opponents, they have to work together as one unit. This is especially crucial for doubles teams, where you have two persons working together as one team against another team of two persons. Since there are only two teammates per team, there is great need of both teammates being in "one accord." This is part of how, in tennis, Serena and Venus Williams were able to win many grand slam doubles titles and Olympics gold medals.

By comparison, marriage is a team of two. It was instituted by God and, among other things, requires mutual honor, mutual respect, mutual submission, love, and sacrifice to make it to the "finish line," and win together.

This may, on different occasions, include giving up or forgoing your rights, needs, and desires to maintain the unity, harmony, and togetherness of the marriage, as you can expect to do in any meaningful relationship. However, this doesn't mean you become a doormat and allow yourself to be walked all over.

With all of that said, remember honor and respect are earned, not demanded or exacted from your husband, wife, children, or anyone else. Now, here are some examples of how you can express love, honor, respect, submission, and sacrifice in your marriage:

by accepting your husband or wife as an individual and not imposing your personality on them; by maintaining a close family circle that discourages outside interferences from others like friends and family; by helping out around the house, though you are the breadwinner; by helping out with baby-caring; by taking out the trash occasionally, though it's primarily your partner's responsibility; by keeping-house; by personal care like showering daily and taking care of your oral hygiene; by laundering your clothes and taking care of your overall health; by including your spouse in the decision-making process concerning the family, especially the family You also love and honor your spouse by not committing psychological or physical abuse on them, and the list can go on and on.

finance. You also love and honor your spouse by not committing psychological or physical abuse on them, and the list can go on and on.

2. Speak each other's love language. (1 John 3:18; Hebrews 10:24)

I spoke of marriage as a team, and there are common interest and activities that bond and unite it's members. One of those elements is speaking a language they all understand, and love is a universal language that both husbands and wives understand. Gary Chapman, the author of *The Five Love Languages*, puts forth the concept that everyone has at least one primary love language.[22] When it is spoken, it speaks more deeply to their emotions and fills up that person's "love tank."

According to Mr. Chapman, the five love languages are Words of Affirmation, Quality Time, Physical Touch, Acts of Service, and Receiving Gifts. Let's look at a brief introduction of each.

1. Words of affirmation

Using words to provide affirmation to your spouse. "You look nice in that dress." "I really appreciate what you did for me." "Do you know one of the things I like about you? Your smile. When you smile at me, the whole world looks beautiful." "One of the things I like about you is

Remember the ancient Hebrew proverb we quoted in chapter 1? "The tongue has the power of life and death."

your integrity. I know that you will always tell me the truth." The words may focus on how they look, something they have done for you, or some personality trait. You are simply using words to express your love. You can speak the words, write the words, or even sing the words. Remember the ancient Hebrew proverb we quoted in chapter 1? "The tongue has the power of life and death."

For some people, Words of Affirmation is their primary love language. If you give them affirming words, they thrive. They feel deeply loved. If, on the other hand, you give them harsh, critical words, it is like a dagger in their heart.[23]

2. Quality time

Giving your spouse your undivided attention. I do not mean sitting on the couch watching television (something else has your attention). Nor do I mean sitting in the same room while both of you are looking at your laptops. I'm talking about things like sitting on the couch or in your favorite chairs, with the television off, computers down, not answering your phones, but rather looking at each other and talking and listening. They have your undivided attention. Or taking a walk and talking as you walk. Or, in your former life, it might have been going to your favorite restaurant, assuming that you were talking

For the person whose love language is Quality Time, what you are doing is not as important as the fact you are doing it together.[24]

and listening to each other. (Maybe that day will return soon.) I have been amazed in the past several years to observe couples sitting in the restaurant with both of them on their smartphones. I hope neither of their love languages is Quality Time.

Quality time also has other dialects, such as doing something together that at least one of you enjoys doing and the other chooses to participate. For the person whose love language is Quality Time, what you are doing is not as important as the fact you are doing it together.[24]

3. Physical touch

Meaningful, affirming touches. In a marriage, this would be such things as holding hands, kissing, embracing, sexual intercourse, placing your hand on their shoulder as you pour their coffee, or putting your hand on their leg as you drive down the road. We have long known the power of physical touch. That is why we cuddle babies in our arms, and long before the baby understands the meaning of love, the baby feels loved by physical touch.[25]

4. Acts of service

Doing something for your spouse that you know they would like for you to do. Cooking a meal is an act of service. Washing dishes, folding towels, watering the lawn, washing the car, or changing

Have you heard the old saying, "Actions speak louder than words"? That is true if Acts of Service is your love language. However, it is not true for everyone.[26]

the baby's diaper are all acts of service. The husband whom I described earlier was speaking this love language. Many wives would feel deeply loved if their husbands did those acts of service. His problem was that he was not married to one of these women. Acts of Service was not his wife's love language. He was, in fact, expressing love, but it was missing the target. Have you heard the old saying, "Actions speak louder than words?" That is true if Acts of Service is your love language. However, it is not true for everyone.[26]

5. Receiving gifts

It is universal to give gifts as an expression of love. My academic background before I studied counseling was cultural anthropology, the study of cultures. We have never discovered a culture where gift giving is not an expression of love. The gift says to the recipient, "They were thinking about me. Look what they got for me."

> The gift need not be expensive. I have sometimes suggested to husbands that they follow the example of their young children who pick dandelions in the yard and give them to their mothers. I'm not suggesting dandelions, but flowers from the yard. If you don't have flowers in your yard, look at your neighbor's yard. (Ask your neighbors; don't steal them.) One husband told me that he was taking a walk and saw a bird feather. He picked it up and took it home and gave it to his wife with these words: "Honey, I found this feather while I was walking, and I thought of you. You are the wind beneath my wings, girl, and I love

you." He hit a home run because his wife's primary love language was Words of Affirmation, and her secondary language was Receiving Gifts.[27]

To conclude this brief introduction of the five love languages, here is what Mr. Chapman has to say in addition:

The love languages are not gender specific. A man or a woman can have any one of the five as their primary love language. The important thing is to discover your spouse's primary love language and choose to speak it on a regular basis. This does not mean that you can ignore the other languages. No, you can sprinkle in the other four for "extra credit." However, if you don't speak your spouse's primary love language, they will not feel loved even though you are speaking some of the other languages.[28]

3. Be a complement and not a competition. (Romans 12:16)

Next to speaking your spouse's love language is being their complement instead of their competition.

There are many things in this world that we find attractive, beautiful, lovely, or pleasing, regardless of their varied differences or characteristics. For example, a musical symphony, a band, or a group of singers have different instruments and voices, but when blended in a complementary manner, they create a beautiful musical symphony. How about another example: the exterior colors of a house can make it more appealing to people because of their contrast; like a baby blue or a baby yellow house with white trimming, or perhaps a brown or gray house with white trimming, generally are complementary colors. At least, here in the West, they are typically seen as such.

Similarly, there are psychological, physiological, and physical differences between men and women, yet they naturally complement each other. However, many couples exude a spirit of competition, which results in strife and disharmony.

For instance, when a wife or husband expresses superiority over each other, they are in competition with each other. When a husband or wife constantly reminds their partner of their failures and inabilities, or seeks to downplay what their husband or wife does and prop themselves up as better, that's a competition, not a complement.

On the other hand, when both husband and wife seek to use their talents and abilities to build up each other, that fosters unity and togetherness in the relationship, and that's complementary.[29]

When a husband or wife constantly reminds their partner of their failures and inabilities, or seeks to downplay what their husband or wife does and prop themselves up as better, that's a competition, not a complement.

When either partners insist that in order for them to be happy, or to maintain unity and harmony in the relationship, their husband or wife has to do everything their way, that's a competition not a complement. However, when both husband and wife consider each other's needs and desires in the operation of the home, and the things they do independently or together, then they are a complement and not in competition with each other.

When both spouses work outside of the home and the first one to get home decides to start dinner, that's a complement, even if that husband or wife who starts dinner is not the one who mainly prepares the meals.

Here is a final one to be careful of, and that is being a "corrector" of your spouse's verbiage or mannerisms, which some wives or husbands believe it's their duty to do. While this evidences the spirit of competition, it also precipitates conflict. Now, once again, there is nothing wrong with correction, but you can exacerbate your husband or wife if you often correct or fix up everything they say or do, or how they say and do what they do.

This can lead to feelings of unacceptance and condescension. Hence you may very well be intruding on their personality.

Now, once again, there is nothing wrong with correction, but you can exacerbate your husband or wife if you often correct or fix up everything they say or do, or how they say and do what they do.

One Bible teaching that supports all that we've been looking at in this section says to put away strife (a prideful or rival spirit), vain glory (conceit, haughty attitude, or high-mindedness), and in humility of mind esteem (honor) each other better than ourselves (less self-focused).[30]

4. Speak verbal balms and not verbal bombs. (Proverbs 16:24; 18:21; James 3:10).

This next item in the marriage decalogue is crucial, for life and death are in the power of the tongue (used to bless and curse). You can tear down your spouse and your marriage with harsh, cruel and condemning words, or you can build it up and give it life by speaking words of affirmation, commendation, and yes, loving correction.

One form of verbal bombing is name-calling. It is done by some couples and is an act of styling your partner with derogatory names (bitch, dog, idiot, whore, stupid, worthless, etc.), whether said in anger or not, it diminishes your husband's or wife's personhood—their value as a person in the relationship. In doing these things, you are building up emotional barriers that you will have to work very hard to tear down later on.

The goal in speaking verbal balms is to speak "pleasant words," words that build up, not tear down, words that encourage, and not discourage, words that are "seasoned" with grace—a balm of healing.[32]

How ever grieved you are about what's going on with your marriage, remember that grievous words stir up anger, and if you both continually "verbal bombing" each other, then you'll eventually become bitter enemies and will ultimately have an all-out war. One thing you can do avoid this is to call a truce on throwing "verbal bombs" and start speaking "verbal balms" instead.

"Verbal balms" should not only be spoken to our spouses but our children as well. "Whenever the mother can speak a word of commendation for the good conduct of her children, she should do so. She should encourage them by words of approval and looks of love. These will be as sunshine to the heart of a child and will lead to the cultivation of self-respect and pride of character."[31] Of course, this should be the course of action taken by the father also. The goal in speaking verbal balms is to speak "pleasant words," words that build up, not tear down, words that encourage, and not discourage, words that are "seasoned" with grace—a balm of healing.[32]

5. Be a role model spouse and parent. (John 13:13-16)

Speaking verbal balms can positively and profoundly impact those you speak them to. But another social dynamic which has a profound impact on relationships is role-modeling. The American Psychology Association states that a role model is "a person or group serving as an exemplar for the goals, attitudes, or behavior of an individual, who identifies with and seeks to imitate the role model."

The glaring reality is that people influence people.

APA dictionary definition of role-modelhttps://dictionary. apa. org/role-model[33] The glaring reality is that people influence people.

The term "influencer" is well known today. One type of "influencer" is "entertainers," like actors (movie stars) and singers, who are sometimes referred to as performing artists. These persons not only influence the thinking of a mass of people but also boost marketing and increase revenues and services they are "branded" or associated with. For example, if you want your children to be clean and organized, you should be clean and organized too.

The idea of being a role-model spouse may be new to you, but how it works is fundamental in human-to-human relationships. As individuals, we speak with certain accents, dress a certain way, and express different hand and facial gestures because these are learned behaviors which we mirror from our family, friends, icons, and other acquaintances. Just take a look at the youth around you, observe the way they speak, act, and dress. Then take a look at the various "influencers" they watch and listen to, as well as the different authorities they associate with, and ask the question, "Which of these persons are the youths emulating?"

Interestingly, this sociological phenomenon is captured in the Bible. In 2 Corinthians 3:18, it tells us that "by beholding, we become changed." What this is telling us is that, what or who we constantly see, hear, and think about affects us philosophically, physiologically, psychologically, and behaviorally. Coupled to this, the Romans 2:21–25 encourages us to be the change we want to see in others (our husbands, wives, or children). In other words, live up to the standard you expect your spouse and others to live up to.[34]

While being a role-model spouse can inspire positive changes in your partner, you should also role model the value system you want to pass on to your children.[35] For example, if you want your children to be clean and organized, you should be clean and organized too.

If you want your children to be mindful and respectful of others, then treat others with courtesy and respect. If you want your children to carry forth a spiritual heritage, then they should see you making spiritual things a priority.

However, keep in mind that children are more impressionable and susceptible to changes than grown-ups are. So you will need to be more patient and tolerant with your spouse than with children; and don't forget, you accepted and marry your partner as they were. So don't go trying to change them now. To reiterate, there is nothing wrong with correction, but you can exacerbate your husband or wife if you often correct or fix up everything they say or do, or how they say or do what they say or do. They may

But remember, the changes in your life can influence your spouse and others around you to change, so once again, be the change you want to see in each other, as well as your children.

feel unaccepted and underappreciated, and you may very well be intruding on them. But remember, the changes in your life can influence your spouse and others around you to change, so once again, be the change you want to see in each other, as well as your children.

6. Make a pledge of purity. (2 Corinthians 7:1; Ephesians 5:3)

So far, we've looked at four of the ten principles in the marriage decalogue. We've looked at being a role-model spouse, speaking verbal balms instead of verbal bombs, being a complement instead of a competition, speaking each other's love language and marriage as a team. But without integrity, all of that will fall to the ground.

Let's get some statistical perspective on this:

> Three in four Americans say they have ever been in a monogamous relationship with someone and 51% say they are currently in a monogamous relationship. While monogamy is generally understood as both partners agreeing not to have any other partners, opinions on what is considered cheating in a monogamous relationship vary. YouGov asked Americans which of 10 hypothetical actions

> This means that many TV shows and movies we watch, music we listen to or books, comics, and magazines we read that encourage impurity and infidelity in marriage will have to be discarded.

they would consider cheating if done by someone who is in a monogamous relationship.

Nine in 10 Americans say that having sex with another person or sending nude photos of oneself to another person is cheating. Majorities of Americans also consider most of the actions listed as cheating, including sending suggestive online messages to another person (83%), lying about spending time with another person (80%), and forming an intense emotional attachment to another person (73%).[36]

So the purity pledge is about maintaining the integrity of your marriage vows. And you can do this by guarding against lust and filtering out unclean and immoral content viewing.[37] This means that many TV shows and movies we watch, music we listen to or books, comics, and magazines we read that encourage impurity and infidelity in marriage will have to be discarded.

Though controversial among many, this also includes, not only fasting from but abstaining from porn and masturbation—*yes*, porn and masturbation interfere with closeness and intimacy in marriage, besides negatively impacting your health.[38]

Additionally, you should not use sex nor money as a weapon or a tool of control and manipulation. This breaks down trust, objectifies your partner and sex, quenches the fires of intimacy, breeds resentment, and leads to marital insecurity and infidelity.

We also maintain the integrity of our marriage by rendering to each other "due benevolence" and minimize long separation as much as possible.[39] "Due benevolence" means, being there for your spouse sexually, as you should, and within reasonability. Yet when our spouse is not able or available to fulfill us sexually, we maintain the integrity of the marriage by being considerate, being patient, and exercising abstinence.

To add to what we've looked at so far, you also maintain the integrity of your marriage by avoiding flirting, jesting, and being careful of how you compliment and receive compliments from others.[40] I once heard someone say they reply to certain compliments by saying, "Thank you, my husband says that to me all the time," or, "Well, thank you, my wife tells me that every day." You may feel uncomfortable to say this, but it does help to defuse inappropriate interactions, thus, maintaining appropriate relational boundaries. Additionally, you should not use sex nor money as a weapon or a tool of control and manipulation. This breaks down trust, objectifies your partner and sex, quenches the fires of intimacy, breeds resentment, and leads to marital insecurity and infidelity.

Lastly, transparency (which is being open and honest without secrecy) is another way to maintain marital fidelity, because secrecy in marriage, paves the road to unfaithfulness, *especially* private and secret relationships.

Please don't mistake transparency to mean that you overwhelm your spouse with every thought you have or actions you commit, or the details of all your conversations with others or expect your spouse to be this way with you. Neither should you mistake transparency to mean that your life and marriage is to be an "open book"—sharing all the details of your married life with others.

Again, transparency means there is no intent to deceive or mislead others about who you are and even your marriage. This allows others who love and care about you and your marriage to "check" your actions; thus, they become accountability partners and help you be accountable to your marriage vows and uphold marriage fidelity.

7. Choose to resolve and not dissolve conflicts. (Romans 12:18)

Indeed, if we are going to maintain marriage fidelity, we also have to manage conflicts accordingly.

Let's start with this excerpt from the book fighting for your marriage:

> It is normal to have conflicts in relationships. People are different, and their desires and needs will inevitably clash. Resolving disagreements in a healthy way creates understanding and brings couples closer together. The objective should be the betterment of the relationship. This is positive conflict.[41]

Marriage and family life counselors emphasize that one of the main keys to resolving conflicts is clear communication. Without open communication, you cannot find real resolutions. When you communicate with your partner, speak to the issue clearly and directly, and do not attack their personhood or their character.

So say what you mean to say about the problem you're confronted with, and let your yes be yes and your no be no.[42]

In other words, be honest in your communication with one another. If you are not able to meet your spouse's expectations within good reason, let them know that. If you are uncomfortable or unhappy about something, especially if they ask you about it, don't say, "I'm fine," "It's okay," "It's nothing," "It's no big deal, really!" "Whatever you decide, I'll go with it." Only to find out later that it is not okay, it is a big deal, and you're neither ok nor fine with "it." Now your husband or wife is deeply disappointed, you find yourself arguing with each other, and before you know it, you have a mountain of issues on your hand and added marital strain.

When you communicate with your partner, speak to the issue clearly and directly, and do not attack their personhood or their character.

Additionally, when we are clear and direct in our communication with each other (not rude, or disrespectful), we leave less room for miscommunications and misunderstandings. This dramatically reduces conflict.

However, sometimes we believe we are putting forth our best efforts to communicate clearly what we mean to say, but misunderstandings may still arise between you both.

This is because people filter what we say to them, and we, likewise, filter what they say to us.

The authors of *Fighting for Your Marriage* states that there are five types of filters couples encounter when communicating with each other:

(1) Distraction

(2) Emotional states

(3) Beliefs and expectations

(4) Differences in styles

(5) Self-protection.[43]

As you read over this list of five conversational filters, you should understand how easily miscommunications can happen. Some spouses are physically present in a conversation, but their minds are still caught up with what's going on at work, church, or school. Some are still focused on the pain of being mistreated by others, perhaps a family member or a close friend. A husband or wife may appear to be smiling on the outside but on the inside is brooding over the many times they have been deeply wounded and disappointed because of what their partner said or unfulfilled expectations they had.

As you read over this list of five conversational filters, you should understand how easily miscommunications can happen.

Now some of this may just
be coming from a place of
insecurity, low self-esteem,
naivety, ignorance, or
arrogance. Yet all of these
social dynamics play into
how we communicate—
what we say or not say
to each other, or how we
say certain things, as well
as how we hear and interpret
what others say to us.

To
emphasize:
Problems usually do not
go away when they are not
dealt with appropriately. They
typically fester and come out in
other forms, like angry outbursts,
bitterness, contempt, heated
arguments, indifference,
resentment, and
even violence.

It doesn't mean that you need to turn off your filters. Just be aware of them and be careful of their potential to ruin your best communication efforts.

Another step in resolving conflict is to avoid prolonged or unnecessary delays in addressing issues.[44] *Yes*, not every problem can be addressed immediately or in one conversation. But if we keep on delaying or "sweeping" the issues under the rug, instead of confronting them (particularly the "small ones"), we'll eventually encounter a "blowout." Because the things we don't work out we'll eventually act out. To emphasize: Problems usually do not go away when they are not dealt with appropriately. They typically fester and come out in other forms, like angry outbursts, bitterness, contempt, heated arguments, indifference, resentment, and even violence.

Just like a blown-out tire on a car, you can only go so far until you have to stop and address the situation to get back on the road safely again.

Note: If you are experiencing physical abuse in your relationship, seek help; do not stay in a physically abusive situation. No relationship is worth being physically abused for. You're of far more value than what that relationship is worth.

You might even need to relinquish your rights and preferences to come to a place of resolution but do not compromise on moral principles.

But by all means necessary, seek to resolve disagreements as soon as possible, especially the "little things."

Certain issues, like some personalities, can be complex and complicated. However, avoiding relationship issue or the person is choosing to dissolve, rather than resolve them. I would say, whether you're dealing with a complicated personality or not, be apologetic in your approach. Regardless of how wrong the other person is, own up to your wrongs; take responsibility for your own words or actions that may have fueled the situation.[45] You might even need to relinquish your rights and preferences to come to a place of resolution but do not compromise on moral principles.

In addition, whether you are dealing with a difficult situation, a complex personality or not, it does help to put aside pride and avoid condescending, contemptuous attitudes or remarks. Just like a soft answer turns away wrath, these are vital steps to getting contention and strife to cease.[46]

8. Choose confrontation and not retaliation. (Matthew 18:15–17)

Relating to number seven of the marriage decalogue is choosing confrontation and not retaliation. This is also a vital step toward conflict resolution.

Conversely, while confrontation tend to have a negative connotation, it is about coming to a place of common understanding and agreement.

We readily understand retaliation to be "payback," or as the "locals" would say, "I clap back." In other words, since you did me wrong, I'm going to get back at you for doing me wrong. With this mindset, you consequently have backstabbing for backstabbing, cheating for cheating, hurt for hurt, insult for insult, indifference for indifference, injury for injury, sarcasm for sarcasm, spite for spite, so on and so forth. Conversely, while confrontation tend to have a negative connotation, it is about coming to a place of common understanding and agreement.

Which can only happen when persons get together to talk about and work through the issues they are faced with.

In her book *Confronting Without Offending*, Deborah Smith Pegues discusses a number of things involving positive and practical steps toward resolving conflict. I want to draw your attention, briefly, to the four confrontation and conflict management styles she writes about, as well as the 5Ps of confrontation she elaborates on.

> True love cannot be won by force or manipulation; only by love is love awakened and respect begets respect.[47]

Let's start with the four confrontation and conflict management styles first:

1. The Dictator: "Do it my way."

2. The Accommodator: "Have it your way."

3. The Abdicator: "I'll run away."

4. The Collaborator: "Let's find a way."

The Dictator – A dictator's way of governance is abhorred by its people. The dictator's approach to conflict resolution does not foster a healthy relationship—one in which each partner has a fair say. The dictators often say, "It's my way or the highway."

The dictator may gain the conformity of those he or she relates to or manages, but not their love or respect. True love cannot be won by force or manipulation; only by love is love awakened and respect begets respect.[47]

The Accommodator – But neither would the accommodator's approach work because one of the two personalities becomes stifled, like in the situation with the dictator. This unbalances the relationship, breeds resentment and dissatisfaction, and unhappiness eventually sets in. The *accommodator* will often say you can have it your way—whatever you want, and may mean well in saying this; however, relationships need "checks" and "balances," and the *accommodator* fall short of fulfilling that role.

The Abdicator – It goes without saying, but the *abdicator's* approach to conflict resolution isn't the best solution either, because running away from people or problems dissolves them instead of resolves them.

Anger, anxiety, bitterness, depression, and resentment follows the abdicator because he or she carries around much emotional baggage from the various circumstances and relationships they run from.

They avoid confrontation at all costs because they see it as a negative interaction, rather than understanding that confrontation is just two people coming together to get to a place of common understanding an agreement.

The Collaborator – Though collaboration is not always easy, it is the better of the four styles of handling conflicts properly.

When confronting your wife or husband, do it Prayerfully, Promptly, Personally, Privately, and Purposefully,[48] says Mrs. Deborah.

You know the old saying: United we stand; divided we fall. Treating each other as equals instead of rivals, recognizing you both have faults and neither of you are perfect, making room for your spouse's input, and strategizing together demonstrates the *collaborator's* conflict management personality style.

While the *collaborator's* approach to conflict resolution is the best, there are appropriate times in which we need to dictate, accommodate, and abdicate. Knowing when the time is right to do either of these is crucial.

Added to the four conflict personality and confrontation styles are the 5Ps of confrontation. When confronting your wife or husband, do it Prayerfully, Promptly, Personally, Privately, and Purposefully,[48] says Mrs. Deborah.

Now, let us take a brief look at each of these Ps.

Prayerfully – We believe that prayer can change circumstances and people. For added emphasis look at what James 5:16 says: "Confess your faults one to another, and pray one for another, that you may be healed. The effective fervent prayer of a righteous man avails much." Though you may not feel or think you're one of them, still pray. In all your ways acknowledge God and He shall direct your paths.[49]

Promptly – I've already mentioned the necessity of addressing problems before they grow into overwhelming mountains. But just to add the old proverb: "There is no time like the present." Yet I haven't forgotten that not all confrontations can take place immediately and not all issues in marriage can be addressed or be resolved at once. Some may not even find a resolution other than agreeing to disagree and moving on with the things that matters more. Just like bad habits, some problems develop over a long period of time, and like bad habits, are overcome over time.

So be patient. But as soon as you have the opportunity to make up, do so. Let not the son go down on your wrath or anger.

Additionally, the longer you wait is the more opportunity there is for misunderstandings and ill-feelings to set in. So when you and or your spouse is in a good headspace, get together and work through the issues you can address.

> Just like bad habits, some problems develop over a long period of time, and like bad habits, are overcome over time.

Personally – While prayer changes things, we have to do our part. This means that you and not your friends or family members should go and address your spouse. In fact, they should not be "wrapped" up in your family affairs. Otherwise, you wind up wounding your spouse. This drives a wedge between you two and fracture family connections. Coming to a place of common understanding with your partner is a personal matter, and it is your personal responsibility. Also, this is part of how you build, bond, and bind together.

Privately – To keep that bond, you would also need to confront them *privately.* This is also related to addressing your wife or husband personally. Too often, husbands or wives air their dirty laundry. Again, these things wound your spouse even more. Remember the marriage circle is a private and sacred one, but not a secretive one: There are times to confide in a third party when necessary. But the point here is, not to go running your mouth about the faults of your wife or husband, and there are those who do this as a way to manipulate their spouse to change or getting what they want.

Let their faults die within the marriage circle. This is a part of the path to "winning" your partner.

Purposefully – Winning your partner is a good purpose for confronting them *prayerfully, promptly, personally, and privately; these* lead to what I believe the ultimate purpose or goal should be—the restoration of the union.[50] So you would need to be intentional in confronting your wife or husband. Take a non-threatening approach—be empathetic, have your speech "seasoned" with grace, and be kind one to another, tender-hearted, forgiving one another.[51]

But the point here is, not to go running your mouth about the faults of your wife or husband, and there are those who do this as a way to manipulate their spouse to change or getting what they want.

By the way, all of these are found in Jesus's teachings on confrontation and can be applied to different types of relationships. In addition to these five confrontation techniques, you may need to involve a third-party appropriately. However, when consulting a third party, it should not be to prove that you or your ways are correct and your spouse's is not. Again, the goal should be for the betterment of the union, to be on one accord with each other, to be reconciled.[52]

9. Have winsome arguments. (James 1:19)

I don't know about you, but when I am having a conversation with my wife, which at times turn into an argument, I am seeking for understanding, and I'm sure she is too.

But is it wrong for married couples to argue, though? Here is what an excerpt from *Psychology Today* has to say about that.

> Arguments aren't necessarily a bad sign. It means differences are surfacing, but in some relationships, differences aren't acknowledged. This may be because either one partner dominates, or because both individuals are merged and don't really know themselves. One or both partners may be sacrificing who they are to please the other. These solutions to differences usually backfire, because they build resentment and passive-aggressive behavior, and closeness and intimacy suffer.[53]

As I mentioned in the section on resolving instead of dissolving conflict, you should attack the issue, not the person. You two are a team and you should see the issues as common threats to the security of your union.[54] However, this doesn't mean you cannot address certain personality factors affecting the marriage, but if you do, be sure to do so with care. Laying out all of your spouse's character defects, shortcomings, and failures before them is not a positive way to tackle conflict. Another vital component to having winsome arguments is not to be too hasty to speak (nor be combative or defensive).

For the person who gives an answer to a matter before he hears it, to him it's folly and shame.[55] So seek first to understand what your partner is communicating, then for them to understand your perspectives.[56] Quite frankly, some of the arguments my wife and I have is because of hasty speech. We at times assume what the other is thinking or about to say and begin to mount our defense before they had an opportunity to finish, or we read into what the other has said and, or we've been anxious to talk about something, so while conversing, arguing, or debating one issue, we throw in the other issue we could hardly wait to discuss. Before you know it, a lot of time and energy is spent in disagreement.

> Another vital component to having winsome arguments is not to be too hasty to speak (nor be combative or defensive).

Giving a "soft answer" does not mean you're a weak person; on the contrary, it takes some level of self-control to give a soft answer, demonstrating strength of character. Neither does giving a "soft answer" means you should suppress your perspectives of the situation you're both faced with. Their needs to be a platform in the relationship to talk freely. Yet there are occasions where we need to pull back. At this point, a "soft answer" may mean "biting your tongue"—not every thought needs to be expressed. At least, not all at once and indeed not all the time we feel impulse to do so. Once again, this is not an indication of weakness but of self-control, demonstrating strength of character.

A "soft answer" May also mean saying sorry today, but talking it over tomorrow. *Especially* when we are too

In addition to not being too hasty to speak, let us practice speaking "soft answers" to turn away wrath (aggravation, irritation), for grievous (inflated) words provoke anger.[57]

passionate and emotional about what we are arguing over that we can't see through the fog clearly. Hence, we need to take a break and cool down to have a clear-focused conversation. The various approaches mentioned in this section has one thing in common: self-control. This is a part of the fruit of the Spirit of God, and thereby, we can find the strength to not only have winsome arguments, but also winsome conversations.

10. Exercise forgiveness and reconciliation. (James 5:16)

Clear-focused conversations are crucial to clear up misunderstandings and is also necessary in the process of forgiveness and reconciliation.

Many people struggle with what forgiveness is, how, and when to forgive. Some recognize a distinction between forgiveness and reconciliation, while others do not; yet, they are different. Reconciliation requires forgiveness, but forgiveness doesn't require reconciliation.

We can extend and experience forgiveness, though we are not reconciled with the other person, but we won't be reconciled to anyone whom we have wronged or have wronged us unless forgiveness is reciprocated.

On the topic of forgiveness and reconciliation, the *Greater Good Magazine*, published online by Berkeley University, says, "Psychologists generally define forgiveness as a conscious, deliberate decision to release feelings of resentment or vengeance toward a person or group who has harmed you, regardless of whether they actually deserve your forgiveness."[58]

This is also what the Bible teaches, and this kind of forgiveness releases us from being consumed with anger, bitterness, resentment, and other negative emotions that wears down our minds and emotions.

> Reconciliation requires forgiveness, but forgiveness doesn't require reconciliation.

The above article further states:

> Just as important as defining what forgiveness *is*, though, is understanding what forgiveness is *not*. Experts who study or teach forgiveness make clear that when you forgive, you do not gloss over or deny the seriousness of an offense against you. Forgiveness does not mean forgetting, nor does it mean condoning or excusing offenses. Though forgiveness can help repair a damaged relationship, it doesn't obligate you to reconcile with the person who harmed you, or release them from legal accountability.[59]

Once again, reconciliation demands a righting of wrongs by, at least, acknowledging and confessing them to the person you've offended, hurt or harmed. Then, wherever possible, make restitution. One restitutionary effort that needs to happen to heal and maintain long-term relationships is the rebuilding of broken trust. However, in some cases, separation is the only healthy form of reconciliation.

With that said, I once heard about a couple going through counseling to reconcile their relationship. The wife said she was encouraged to express fully how she felt about her husband. Without reservation, she "blasted" her husband during the counseling session. "Well, she got it out of her system," you may say. However, looking back at this experience, she admitted that was poor counsel she was given, which she regretted following. Imagine how that can devastate a husband or a wife; imagine how much more that would fracture a marriage on the verge of collapse. In fact, she mentioned that the after-effects lasted for many years. If you feel the need to vent your anger, bitterness, disappointment, or frustration toward the person who has hurt you in order for you to forgive them, then, you're not ready to forgive, and you won't sincerely forgive unless you have a change of heart.

If you feel the need to vent your anger, bitterness, disappointment, or frustration toward the person who has hurt you in order for you to forgive them, then, you're not ready to forgive, and you won't sincerely forgive unless you have a change of heart.

Now, don't misunderstand me: It is not wrong to say to your spouse, "I was angry for what you did or said, but I forgive you." That is different from saying, "I hate you; you are the scum of the earth; you're the worst; I wish I was not married to you, but I am willing to forgive you for what you did to me." Now how would you feel if your partner says this to you?

Furthermore, this does more damage as it's an attack on the person instead of addressing the issues in particular.

How about adopting these biblical, practical approaches toward forgiveness and even reconciliation instead: Don't go to bed angry; make up as soon as you can.[60] Be kind, tenderhearted, and forgiving to each other.[61] Confess your faults one to another (not the faults of you wife or husband) and pray for each other. This makes room for reconciliation and healing.[62] Therefore, making peace, and peacemaking fosters right actions.[63] Right actions encourage, strengthen, and rebuild broken connections in our relationships.

EPILOGUE (Summary)

Marriages go through various stages, but all do not progress through the five predictable stages to the same degree of intensity. With mutual respect, mutual submission, mutual honor, love, and sacrifice, husbands and wives can better navigate the contours of marriage. As we navigate our way, we don't always see eye to eye, yet let us be there for each other. In loving cooperation, let us find a way to resolve conflicts, build each other up with our words, and not tear each other down: Call a truce on verbal bombs by speaking loving, affirming, empathetic words to each other. It is often easy to throw verbal bombs as it is to point a finger at someone else. However, the challenge to us is to be an example of the person we want our spouse and children to be. Let your speech be "seasoned" with grace as you confront each other about the issues you're both faced with in the marriage, and seek first to understand your spouse's point of view before trying to get them to understand yours. At times this may still turn into an argument, but arguments aren't necessarily bad, and though we argue with each other, we still need to listen to what the other person is saying, though angry, passionate, or upset. Sometimes we argue, combat, and defend ourselves instead of humbly admitting to faults; when if we confess our faults one to another and pray for each other, our marriages would experience healing. This healing is also necessary for reconciliation, but not without first extending and experiencing forgiveness. Remember, you can forgive someone even if they do not change or seek your forgiveness. Once again, as you "release" that person from the wrong they've done to you, you also release yourself from being consumed with anger, bitterness, resentment, and other negative emotions. While reconciliation requires forgiveness, it also requires you to confront your offender or be confronted by the one you have offended. Finally, if your marriage is going to work out, then you have to *work out* your marriage. For what we don't work out, we'll eventually act out. *Sure*, this is easier said than done, but it can be done, has been done, and is being done by many others.

By God's grace, this can also be your experience and mine.

REFERENCES

1. Gary Chapman, *The 5 Love Languages: Keeping the Love Tank Full*, p. 19, (1992–2015).

2. Proverbs 11:14; 15:22 (KJV).

3. Amos 3:3 (NKJV).

4. Roger K Allen, PhD. *Creating a Happy Marriage and Loving Relationship: Stages of Marriage Satisfaction*, Presentation 3.

5. https://www.usatoday.com/picture-gallery/travel/ destinations/2018/12/20/honeytrek-couple- worldslongest-honeymoon/2373446002/#:~:text= Cusco%20 in%20Peru.-,HoneyTrek,HoneyTrek.

6. https://www.honeytrek.com/about/.

7. Eph. 4:2–3, 32 (KJV).

8. *Fighting for Your Marriage*, page 25–26. (2010).

9. Proverbs 18:22 (KJV).

10. Psalm 37:4 (KJV).

11. *Four Seasons of Marriage*, page 22, par 2. (2005).

12. Ephesians 4:26 (KJV).

13. Revelation 2:4–5 (KJV).

14. James 3:18 (KJV).

15. *Fighting for Your Marriage: Playing Together*, page 258. (2010).

16. Revelation 3:2, 3 (KJV).

17. Ephesians 4:32 (KJV).

18. Proverbs 18:21 (KJV).

19. Gary Chapman, *5 Simple Ways to Strength Your Marriage: Call a Truce on Throwing Verbal Bombs*, page 11. (2020).

20. Colossians 4:6 (KJV).

21. Ellen G. White, *Adventist Home*, page 50.

22. *5 Simple Ways to Strengthen Your Marriage: Discover and Speak Each Other's Love Language*, page 44. (2020).

23. Gary Chapman, *The 5 Love Languages: Words of Affirmation*, chapter 4, page 37–54. (2015).

24. Gary Chapman, *The 5 Love Languages: Quality Time*, chapter 4, page 55–74. (2015).

25. Gary Chapman, *The 5 Love Languages: Physical Touch*, chapter 4, page 107–117. (2015).

26. Gary Chapman, *The 5 Love Languages: Acts of Services*, chapter 4, page 90–106. (2015).

27. Gary Chapman, *The 5 Love Languages: Receiving Gifts*, chapter 4, page 75–89. (2015).

28. Gary Chapman, *5 Simple Ways to Strengthen Your Marriage: Discover and Speak Each Other's Love Language*, page 40–46. (2020).

29. Ephesians 4:7–14 (KJV).

30. Phlipians 2:3–4 (KJV).

31. Volume 1, *Mind Character and Personality*, page 145.

32. Proverbs 16:14; Colossians 4:6 (KJV).

33. https://dictionary.apa.org/role-model.

34. John 13:14, 15; Matt. 7:1–5 (KJV).

35. Deuteronomy. 6:7–9 (KJV).

36. https://today.yougov.com/society/articles/43605-howmany-americans-have-cheated-their-partner-poll.

37. Psalm 101:3; Matthew 5:28 (KJV).

38. Matthew 5:29–30; Philippians 2:8; 2 Corinthians 7:1 (KJV).

39. 1 Corinthians 7:1–5 (KJV).

40. Ephesians 4:25, 29 (KJV).

41. *How to Handle Conflict Effectively*, February 19, 2020, Darlene Lancer, JD, LMFT https://www.psychologytoday. com/us/blog/toxic-relationships/202002/how-handleconflict-effectively.

42. Isaiah 1:18; Matthew 5:37 (KJV).

43. Howard J. Marksman, Scott M. Stanley, Susan L. Blumberg, *Fighting for Your Marriage*: chapter 4, "When What You Heard Is Not What I Said," page 91–103. (2010).

44. Matthew 5:24, 26. (KJV).

45. James 5:16 (KJV).

46. Proverbs 13:10; 22:10. (KJV).

47. 1 John4:19. (KJV).

48. Debra Smith Pagues, *Confronting Without Offending: Winning with Deborah* (July 22, 2018) https://youtu. be/Zd7L9W8G_Io.

49. Proverbs 3:5 (KJV).

50. Galatians 6:1 (KJV).

51. Ephesians 4:32 (KJV).

52. Matthew 18:15–17; Galatians 6:1 (KJV).

53. *How to Handle Conflict Effectively*, February 19, 2020, Darlene Lancer, JD, LMFT https://

www.psychologytoday. com/us/blog/toxic-relationships/202002/how-handleconflict-effectively.

54. Ecclesiastes. 4:9, 12 (KJV).

55. Proverbs 18:13 (KJV).

56. James 1:19 (KJV).

57. Proverbs 15:1 (KJV).

58. https://greatergood.berkeley.edu/topic/forgiveness/definition#:~:text=I%20Cultivate%20It%3F-,What%20 Is%20Forgiveness%3F,they%20 actually%20 deserve%20your%20forgiveness.

59. https://greatergood.berkeley.edu/topic/forgiveness/definition#:~:text=I%20Cultivate%20It%3F-,What%20 Is%20Forgiveness%3F,they%20 actually%20 deserve%20your%20forgiveness.

60. Ephesians 4:26 (KJV).

61. Ephesians 4:32 (KJV).

62. James 5:16 (KJV).

63. James 3:18 (KJV).

www.ingramcontent.com/pod-product-compliance
Lightning Source LLC
Chambersburg PA
CBHW051555120626
46551CB00013B/1535